Program Your Mind, Achieve Your Desires

Millionaire Mind Programming Daily Planner

By John Alexander

Millionaire Mind Programming

Daily Planner

The author may be contacted at his Website
www.JohnAlexander.com

Published by GrayStone Productions
Printed in the USA

Why You Need to Use the Planner

Congratulations, you hold in your hands, a tool that is capable of changing your entire future. It is a tool that can program your mind to deliver you anything, anyone, take you anywhere, or give you any kind of lifestyle that you can conceive.

What is it that makes some people successful and financially secure in their life while others seem to just limp along? I spent a life-time learning the secrets to achieving goals and having the lifestyle very few achieve. I have pulled information from both my own experiences as well as by observing the many clients I have coached over the years.

How you program your brain is going to show up in your current living condition. Whatever way you live now is exactly what YOU or someone you allowed, to program your mind to create.

Programming your mind is about moving switches on and off, that's why you can be a high school drop-out, just out of prison, just fired, or laid off at one place in your life and a multi-millionaire living the Dream in another.

Your brain is just a hard-drive, nothing more. It will accept any software (mind programs) you plug into it. It will take in a fiction of reality just as easy as truthful reality. In the end, it makes everything you programmed it with, a FACT. Its purpose is to create. And it can only create what it's programmed to create.

There are many ways to reprogram your mind which I covered in detail in my book "Millionaire Mind Programming" available at Amazon. But independent of that book, this Book will change your life over the next 60 days. Fill out the pages each day, 7 days a week. In 3 days you are going to be seeing a new you. In 60 days, anything is possible.

The far easiest and fastest way to program your mind is by writing down key information daily. The rhythm of writing it down daily has been used for many years by those in the know about mind programming. What I bring to the table is a more comprehensive method which ties your entire day into the daily programming.

How to Use the Planner

What I discovered is that by combining my long term goals, with my immediate goals, and further with my list of things I need and want to do that day, a synergy is created that forces the creation of all the things on that page. My long term goals suddenly started lining up with my immediate goals and my daily To-Do list. My daily To-Do list started forming to make my longer term goals happen. Magic happened when I started using this new combination. Note: all goals should be written as if you have them already. See my Best Selling Amazon book "Millionaire Mind Programming" to find out why.

Once you start using this Mind and Daily Planner, you will see immediate changes in your thoughts and actions. You will get laser focused and won't deviate on direction. Changing course wastes so much time when you really just need to keep on the planned course. Let this Planner be your rudder to helping you focus on what you really want, and program your mind to achieve it.

EXAMPLE:

Date: _6-2-2015_   Millionaire Daily Planner

My Long Term Goals

_____ I have $5 Million in the Bank and Real Estate holdings _____

_____ I own 200 properties cashflowing $200 plus profit per month _____

Weekly & Monthly Goals _____ I buy 3 properties a week, every week, I mail out 150 mail pieces a week _____

_____ I exercise 30 minutes 4 times a week, _____ I lost 20 pounds _____

_____ I call back sellers within 30 minutes of their calling me _____

What I Will Start or Do Today

_____ Work on Ads _____

_____ Work on seller files _____

_____ Call Horton back before 5:00pm _____

_____ File Memos at County Clerks Office _____

_____ Mail must go out by 4:00 _____

_____ Devote time to the MM Page _____

_____ Complete the introduction _____

What I Will Stop Today _____ stacking paperwork and letting it get get messy around my desk Making excuses not to exercise, _____

_____ Putting off mailings until the next morning _____

Today's Improvement (What I want to improve) _____ Organization _____

Today's Mind Program Affirmation _____ I keep my office neat, orderly, and everything in its place _____

What I didn't do today that I should have done (*Fill out at end of day*)

_____ Did not work on ads, _____

What I will Do This Week

_____ Call Gary to arrange to see the land and formalize a contract in person. _____

What am I? _I'm a millionaire, I'm neat and orderly, I help baby boomers secure their retirement_
I'm in Great shape
I'm the best buyer a seller can sell to and a retail buyer can by from.

Date:_____   Millionaire Daily Planner

My Long Term Goals

_____
_____
_____

Weekly & Monthly Goals_____
_____
_____
_____

What I Will Start or Do Today

_____
_____
_____
_____
_____
_____
_____
_____
_____
_____
_____
_____
_____
_____

What I Will Stop Today_____
_____
_____

Today's Improvement (What I want to improve) _____
_____

Today's Mind Program Affirmation _____
_____

What I didn't do today that I should have done

_____
_____
_____
_____

What I will Do This Week

_____
_____
_____
_____

What am I? _____
_____
_____
_____

Date:_____ Millionaire Daily Planner

My Long Term Goals

_____
_____
_____

Weekly & Monthly Goals_____
_____
_____
_____

What I Will Start or Do Today

_____
_____
_____
_____
_____
_____
_____
_____
_____
_____
_____
_____
_____
_____
_____

What I Will Stop Today_____
_____
_____

Today's Improvement (What I want to improve) _____
_____
Today's Mind Program Affirmation _____
_____

What I didn't do today that I should have done

_____
_____
_____
_____

What I will Do This Week

_____
_____
_____
_____

What am I? _____
_____
_____
_____

Date:_____   Millionaire Daily Planner

My Long Term Goals

_____
_____
_____

Weekly & Monthly Goals_____
_____
_____
_____

What I Will Start or Do Today

_____
_____
_____
_____
_____
_____
_____
_____
_____
_____
_____
_____
_____
_____

What I Will Stop Today_____
_____
_____

Today's Improvement (What I want to improve) _____
_____

Today's Mind Program Affirmation _____
_____

What I didn't do today that I should have done

_____
_____
_____

What I will Do This Week

_____
_____
_____
_____

What am I? _____
_____
_____
_____

Date:_____   Millionaire Daily Planner

My Long Term Goals

_____
_____
_____

Weekly & Monthly Goals_____
_____
_____
_____

What I Will Start or Do Today

_____
_____
_____
_____
_____
_____
_____
_____
_____
_____
_____
_____
_____

What I Will Stop Today_____
_____
_____

Today's Improvement (What I want to improve) _____
_____

Today's Mind Program Affirmation _____
_____
_____

What I didn't do today that I should have done

_____
_____
_____
_____

What I will Do This Week

_____
_____
_____
_____

What am I? _____
_____
_____
_____

Date:_____   Millionaire Daily Planner

My Long Term Goals

_____
_____
_____

Weekly & Monthly Goals_____
_____
_____
_____

What I Will Start or Do Today

_____
_____
_____
_____
_____
_____
_____
_____
_____
_____
_____
_____

What I Will Stop Today_____
_____
_____

Today's NSP (What I want to improve) _____
_____

Today's Mind Program Affirmation _____
_____

What I didn't do today that I should have done

_____
_____
_____
_____

What I will Do This Week

_____
_____
_____
_____

What am I? _____
_____
_____
_____

Date:_____   Millionaire Daily Planner

My Long Term Goals

_____
_____
_____

Weekly & Monthly Goals_____
_____
_____
_____

What I Will Start or Do Today

_____
_____
_____
_____
_____
_____
_____
_____
_____
_____
_____
_____
_____
_____
_____

What I Will Stop Today_____
_____
_____

Today's NSP (What I want to improve) _____
_____

Today's Mind Program Affirmation _____
_____

What I didn't do today that I should have done

_____
_____
_____

What I will Do This Week

_____
_____
_____
_____

What am I? _____
_____
_____
_____

Date:_____   Millionaire Daily Planner

My Long Term Goals

_____
_____
_____

Weekly & Monthly Goals_____
_____
_____
_____

What I Will Start or Do Today

_____
_____
_____
_____
_____
_____
_____
_____
_____
_____
_____
_____
_____

What I Will Stop Today_____
_____
_____

Today's NSP (What I want to improve) _____
_____

Today's Mind Program Affirmation _____
_____

What I didn't do today that I should have done

_____
_____
_____
_____

What I will Do This Week

_____
_____
_____
_____

What am I? _____
_____
_____
_____

Date:_____   Millionaire Daily Planner

My Long Term Goals

_____
_____
_____

Weekly & Monthly Goals_____
_____
_____
_____

What I Will Start or Do Today

_____
_____
_____
_____
_____
_____
_____
_____
_____
_____
_____
_____
_____

What I Will Stop Today_____
_____
_____

Today's NSP (What I want to improve) _____
_____

Today's Mind Program Affirmation _____
_____

What I didn't do today that I should have done

_____
_____
_____
_____

What I will Do This Week

_____
_____
_____
_____

What am I? _____
_____
_____
_____

Date:_____   Millionaire Daily Planner

My Long Term Goals

_____
_____
_____

Weekly & Monthly Goals_____
_____
_____
_____

What I Will Start or Do Today

_____
_____
_____
_____
_____
_____
_____
_____
_____
_____
_____
_____
_____
_____

What I Will Stop Today_____
_____
_____

Today's NSP (What I want to improve) _____
_____
Today's Mind Program Affirmation _____
_____

What I didn't do today that I should have done

_____
_____
_____
_____

What I will Do This Week

_____
_____
_____
_____

What am I? _____
_____
_____
_____

Date:_____   Millionaire Daily Planner

My Long Term Goals

_____
_____
_____

Weekly & Monthly Goals_____
_____
_____
_____

What I Will Start or Do Today

_____
_____
_____
_____
_____
_____
_____
_____
_____
_____
_____
_____
_____
_____
_____

What I Will Stop Today_____
_____
_____

Today's NSP (What I want to improve) _____
_____

Today's Mind Program Affirmation _____
_____

What I didn't do today that I should have done

_____
_____
_____

What I will Do This Week

_____
_____
_____
_____

What am I? _____
_____
_____
_____

Date:_____   Millionaire Daily Planner

My Long Term Goals

_____
_____
_____

Weekly & Monthly Goals_____
_____
_____
_____

What I Will Start or Do Today

_____
_____
_____
_____
_____
_____
_____
_____
_____
_____
_____
_____
_____
_____
_____

What I Will Stop Today_____
_____
_____

Today's NSP (What I want to improve) _____
_____

Today's Mind Program Affirmation _____
_____

What I didn't do today that I should have done

_____
_____
_____

What I will Do This Week

_____
_____
_____
_____

What am I? _____
_____
_____
_____

Date:_____   Millionaire Daily Planner

My Long Term Goals

_____
_____
_____

Weekly & Monthly Goals_____
_____
_____
_____

What I Will Start or Do Today

_____
_____
_____
_____
_____
_____
_____
_____
_____
_____
_____
_____
_____

What I Will Stop Today_____
_____
_____

Today's NSP (What I want to improve) _____
_____

Today's Mind Program Affirmation _____
_____

What I didn't do today that I should have done

_____
_____
_____
_____

What I will Do This Week

_____
_____
_____
_____

What am I? _____
_____
_____
_____

Date:_____   Millionaire Daily Planner

My Long Term Goals

_____
_____
_____

Weekly & Monthly Goals_____
_____
_____
_____

What I Will Start or Do Today

_____
_____
_____
_____
_____
_____
_____
_____
_____
_____
_____
_____
_____
_____

What I Will Stop Today_____
_____
_____

Today's NSP (What I want to improve) _____
_____
Today's Mind Program Affirmation _____
_____

What I didn't do today that I should have done

_____
_____
_____
_____

What I will Do This Week

_____
_____
_____
_____

What am I? _____
_____
_____
_____

Date:_____   Millionaire Daily Planner

My Long Term Goals
_____
_____
_____

Weekly & Monthly Goals_____
_____
_____
_____

What I Will Start or Do Today
_____
_____
_____
_____
_____
_____
_____
_____
_____
_____
_____
_____
_____
_____

What I Will Stop Today_____
_____
_____

Today's NSP (What I want to improve) _____
_____

Today's Mind Program Affirmation _____
_____

What I didn't do today that I should have done
_____
_____
_____
_____

What I will Do This Week
_____
_____
_____
_____

What am I? _____
_____
_____
_____

Date:_____   Millionaire Daily Planner

My Long Term Goals

_____
_____
_____

Weekly & Monthly Goals_____
_____
_____
_____

What I Will Start or Do Today

_____
_____
_____
_____
_____
_____
_____
_____
_____
_____
_____
_____
_____
_____

What I Will Stop Today_____
_____
_____

Today's NSP (What I want to improve) _____
_____

Today's Mind Program Affirmation _____
_____

What I didn't do today that I should have done

_____
_____
_____
_____

What I will Do This Week

_____
_____
_____
_____

What am I? _____
_____
_____
_____

Date:_____   Millionaire Daily Planner

My Long Term Goals

_____
_____
_____

Weekly & Monthly Goals_____
_____
_____
_____

What I Will Start or Do Today

_____
_____
_____
_____
_____
_____
_____
_____
_____
_____
_____
_____
_____

What I Will Stop Today_____
_____
_____

Today's NSP (What I want to improve) _____
_____

Today's Mind Program Affirmation _____
_____

What I didn't do today that I should have done

_____
_____
_____
_____

What I will Do This Week

_____
_____
_____
_____

What am I? _____
_____
_____
_____

Date:_____   Millionaire Daily Planner

My Long Term Goals
_____
_____
_____

Weekly & Monthly Goals_____
_____
_____
_____

What I Will Start or Do Today
_____
_____
_____
_____
_____
_____
_____
_____
_____
_____
_____
_____
_____
_____

What I Will Stop Today_____
_____
_____

Today's NSP (What I want to improve) _____
_____
Today's Mind Program Affirmation _____
_____

What I didn't do today that I should have done
_____
_____
_____
_____

What I will Do This Week
_____
_____
_____
_____

What am I? _____
_____
_____
_____

Date:_____   Millionaire Daily Planner

My Long Term Goals

_____
_____

Weekly & Monthly Goals_____
_____
_____
_____

What I Will Start or Do Today

_____
_____
_____
_____
_____
_____
_____
_____
_____
_____
_____
_____
_____

What I Will Stop Today_____
_____
_____

Today's NSP (What I want to improve) _____
_____
Today's Mind Program Affirmation _____
_____

What I didn't do today that I should have done

_____
_____
_____

What I will Do This Week

_____
_____
_____
_____

What am I? _____
_____
_____
_____

Date:_____   Millionaire Daily Planner

My Long Term Goals

_____
_____
_____

Weekly & Monthly Goals_____
_____
_____
_____
_____

What I Will Start or Do Today

_____
_____
_____
_____
_____
_____
_____
_____
_____
_____
_____
_____
_____

What I Will Stop Today_____
_____
_____

Today's NSP (What I want to improve) _____
_____

Today's Mind Program Affirmation _____
_____
_____

What I didn't do today that I should have done

_____
_____
_____

What I will Do This Week

_____
_____
_____
_____

What am I? _____
_____
_____
_____

Date:_____   Millionaire Daily Planner

My Long Term Goals

_____
_____
_____

Weekly & Monthly Goals_____
_____
_____
_____

What I Will Start or Do Today

_____
_____
_____
_____
_____
_____
_____
_____
_____
_____
_____
_____
_____

What I Will Stop Today_____
_____
_____

Today's NSP (What I want to improve) _____
_____

Today's Mind Program Affirmation _____
_____
_____

What I didn't do today that I should have done

_____
_____
_____
_____

What I will Do This Week

_____
_____
_____
_____

What am I? _____
_____
_____
_____

Date:_____   Millionaire Daily Planner

My Long Term Goals
_____
_____
_____

Weekly & Monthly Goals_____
_____
_____
_____

What I Will Start or Do Today
_____
_____
_____
_____
_____
_____
_____
_____
_____
_____
_____
_____
_____
_____
_____

What I Will Stop Today_____
_____
_____

Today's NSP (What I want to improve) _____
_____
Today's Mind Program Affirmation _____
_____

What I didn't do today that I should have done
_____
_____
_____
_____

What I will Do This Week
_____
_____
_____
_____

What am I? _____
_____
_____
_____

Date:_____   Millionaire Daily Planner

My Long Term Goals

_____

_____

_____

Weekly & Monthly Goals_____

_____

_____

_____

What I Will Start or Do Today

_____

_____

_____

_____

_____

_____

_____

_____

_____

_____

_____

_____

_____

_____

_____

What I Will Stop Today_____

_____

_____

Today's NSP (What I want to improve) _____

Today's Mind Program Affirmation _____

_____

What I didn't do today that I should have done

_____

_____

_____

_____

What I will Do This Week

_____

_____

_____

_____

What am I? _____

_____

_____

_____

Date:_____   Millionaire Daily Planner

My Long Term Goals

_____
_____
_____

Weekly & Monthly Goals_____
_____
_____
_____

What I Will Start or Do Today

_____
_____
_____
_____
_____
_____
_____
_____
_____
_____
_____
_____
_____
_____

What I Will Stop Today_____
_____
_____
_____

Today's NSP (What I want to improve) _____
_____

Today's Mind Program Affirmation _____
_____

What I didn't do today that I should have done

_____
_____
_____
_____

What I will Do This Week

_____
_____
_____
_____

What am I? _____
_____
_____
_____

Date:_____   Millionaire Daily Planner

My Long Term Goals

_____
_____

Weekly & Monthly Goals_____
_____
_____
_____

What I Will Start or Do Today

_____
_____
_____
_____
_____
_____
_____
_____
_____
_____
_____
_____
_____
_____

What I Will Stop Today_____
_____
_____

Today's NSP (What I want to improve) _____
_____

Today's Mind Program Affirmation _____
_____

What I didn't do today that I should have done

_____
_____
_____
_____

What I will Do This Week

_____
_____
_____
_____

What am I? _____
_____
_____
_____

Date:_____   Millionaire Daily Planner

My Long Term Goals

_____
_____
_____

Weekly & Monthly Goals_____
_____
_____
_____

What I Will Start or Do Today

_____
_____
_____
_____
_____
_____
_____
_____
_____
_____
_____
_____
_____
_____

What I Will Stop Today_____
_____
_____

Today's NSP (What I want to improve) _____
_____

Today's Mind Program Affirmation _____
_____

What I didn't do today that I should have done

_____
_____
_____

What I will Do This Week

_____
_____
_____
_____

What am I? _____
_____
_____
_____

Date:_____ Millionaire Daily Planner

My Long Term Goals

_____
_____
_____

Weekly & Monthly Goals_____
_____
_____
_____

What I Will Start or Do Today

_____
_____
_____
_____
_____
_____
_____
_____
_____
_____
_____
_____
_____
_____

What I Will Stop Today_____
_____
_____

Today's NSP (What I want to improve) _____
_____

Today's Mind Program Affirmation _____
_____

What I didn't do today that I should have done

_____
_____
_____

What I will Do This Week

_____
_____
_____
_____

What am I? _____
_____
_____
_____

Date:_____   Millionaire Daily Planner

My Long Term Goals

_____
_____
_____

Weekly & Monthly Goals_____

_____
_____
_____

What I Will Start or Do Today

_____
_____
_____
_____
_____
_____
_____
_____
_____
_____
_____
_____
_____

What I Will Stop Today_____

_____
_____

Today's NSP (What I want to improve) _____
_____

Today's Mind Program Affirmation _____
_____

What I didn't do today that I should have done

_____
_____
_____

What I will Do This Week

_____
_____
_____

What am I? _____

_____
_____
_____

Date:_____   Millionaire Daily Planner

My Long Term Goals

_____
_____
_____

Weekly & Monthly Goals_____
_____
_____
_____

What I Will Start or Do Today

_____
_____
_____
_____
_____
_____
_____
_____
_____
_____
_____
_____
_____

What I Will Stop Today_____
_____
_____

Today's NSP (What I want to improve) _____
_____

Today's Mind Program Affirmation _____
_____

What I didn't do today that I should have done

_____
_____
_____
_____

What I will Do This Week

_____
_____
_____
_____

What am I? _____
_____
_____
_____

Date:_____   Millionaire Daily Planner

My Long Term Goals

_____
_____
_____

Weekly & Monthly Goals_____
_____
_____
_____

What I Will Start or Do Today

_____
_____
_____
_____
_____
_____
_____
_____
_____
_____
_____
_____
_____
_____

What I Will Stop Today_____
_____
_____

Today's NSP (What I want to improve) _____
_____

Today's Mind Program Affirmation _____
_____

What I didn't do today that I should have done

_____
_____
_____
_____

What I will Do This Week

_____
_____
_____
_____

What am I? _____
_____
_____
_____

Date:_____   Millionaire Daily Planner

My Long Term Goals

_____
_____
_____

Weekly & Monthly Goals_____
_____
_____
_____

What I Will Start or Do Today

_____
_____
_____
_____
_____
_____
_____
_____
_____
_____
_____
_____
_____
_____

What I Will Stop Today_____
_____
_____

Today's NSP (What I want to improve) _____
_____

Today's Mind Program Affirmation _____
_____

What I didn't do today that I should have done

_____
_____
_____
_____

What I will Do This Week

_____
_____
_____
_____

What am I? _____
_____
_____
_____

Date:_____   Millionaire Daily Planner

My Long Term Goals

_____
_____
_____

Weekly & Monthly Goals_____
_____
_____
_____

What I Will Start or Do Today

_____
_____
_____
_____
_____
_____
_____
_____
_____
_____
_____
_____
_____
_____

What I Will Stop Today_____
_____
_____

Today's NSP (What I want to improve) _____
_____

Today's Mind Program Affirmation _____
_____

What I didn't do today that I should have done

_____
_____
_____
_____

What I will Do This Week

_____
_____
_____
_____

What am I? _____
_____
_____
_____

Date:_____   Millionaire Daily Planner

My Long Term Goals

_____
_____
_____

Weekly & Monthly Goals_____

_____
_____
_____

What I Will Start or Do Today

_____
_____
_____
_____
_____
_____
_____
_____
_____
_____
_____
_____
_____
_____

What I Will Stop Today_____

_____
_____

Today's NSP (What I want to improve) _____
_____

Today's Mind Program Affirmation _____
_____

What I didn't do today that I should have done

_____
_____
_____
_____

What I will Do This Week

_____
_____
_____
_____

What am I? _____

_____
_____
_____

Date:_____   Millionaire Daily Planner

My Long Term Goals
_____
_____

Weekly & Monthly Goals_____
_____
_____
_____

What I Will Start or Do Today
_____
_____
_____
_____
_____
_____
_____
_____
_____
_____
_____
_____
_____
_____

What I Will Stop Today_____
_____
_____

Today's NSP (What I want to improve) _____
_____

Today's Mind Program Affirmation _____
_____

What I didn't do today that I should have done
_____
_____
_____
_____

What I will Do This Week
_____
_____
_____
_____

What am I? _____
_____
_____
_____

Date:_____   Millionaire Daily Planner

My Long Term Goals

_____
_____
_____

Weekly & Monthly Goals_____
_____
_____
_____

What I Will Start or Do Today

_____
_____
_____
_____
_____
_____
_____
_____
_____
_____
_____
_____
_____
_____

What I Will Stop Today_____
_____
_____

Today's NSP (What I want to improve) _____
_____

Today's Mind Program Affirmation _____
_____

What I didn't do today that I should have done

_____
_____
_____
_____

What I will Do This Week

_____
_____
_____
_____

What am I? _____
_____
_____
_____

Date:_____   Millionaire Daily Planner

My Long Term Goals

_____
_____
_____

Weekly & Monthly Goals_____
_____
_____
_____

What I Will Start or Do Today

_____
_____
_____
_____
_____
_____
_____
_____
_____
_____
_____
_____

What I Will Stop Today_____
_____
_____

Today's NSP (What I want to improve) _____
_____

Today's Mind Program Affirmation _____
_____

What I didn't do today that I should have done

_____
_____
_____

What I will Do This Week

_____
_____
_____

What am I? _____
_____
_____
_____

Date:_____   Millionaire Daily Planner

My Long Term Goals

_____
_____
_____

Weekly & Monthly Goals_____
_____
_____
_____

What I Will Start or Do Today

_____
_____
_____
_____
_____
_____
_____
_____
_____
_____
_____
_____
_____
_____

What I Will Stop Today_____
_____
_____

Today's NSP (What I want to improve) _____
_____
Today's Mind Program Affirmation _____
_____

What I didn't do today that I should have done

_____
_____
_____
_____

What I will Do This Week

_____
_____
_____
_____

What am I? _____
_____
_____
_____

Date:_____   Millionaire Daily Planner

My Long Term Goals

_____
_____
_____

Weekly & Monthly Goals_____
_____
_____
_____

What I Will Start or Do Today

_____
_____
_____
_____
_____
_____
_____
_____
_____
_____
_____
_____
_____

What I Will Stop Today_____
_____
_____

Today's NSP (What I want to improve) _____
_____

Today's Mind Program Affirmation _____
_____

What I didn't do today that I should have done

_____
_____
_____
_____

What I will Do This Week

_____
_____
_____
_____

What am I? _____
_____
_____
_____

Date:_____   Millionaire Daily Planner

My Long Term Goals

_____
_____
_____

Weekly & Monthly Goals_____
_____
_____
_____

What I Will Start or Do Today

_____
_____
_____
_____
_____
_____
_____
_____
_____
_____
_____
_____
_____

What I Will Stop Today_____
_____
_____

Today's NSP (What I want to improve) _____
_____

Today's Mind Program Affirmation _____
_____

What I didn't do today that I should have done

_____
_____
_____
_____

What I will Do This Week

_____
_____
_____
_____

What am I? _____
_____
_____
_____

Date:_____   Millionaire Daily Planner

My Long Term Goals

_____
_____

Weekly & Monthly Goals_____
_____
_____
_____

What I Will Start or Do Today

_____
_____
_____
_____
_____
_____
_____
_____
_____
_____
_____
_____

What I Will Stop Today_____
_____
_____

Today's NSP (What I want to improve) _____
_____

Today's Mind Program Affirmation _____
_____

What I didn't do today that I should have done

_____
_____
_____

What I will Do This Week

_____
_____
_____

What am I? _____
_____
_____
_____

Date:_____   Millionaire Daily Planner

My Long Term Goals
_____
_____
_____

Weekly & Monthly Goals_____
_____
_____
_____

What I Will Start or Do Today
_____
_____
_____
_____
_____
_____
_____
_____
_____
_____
_____
_____
_____
_____

What I Will Stop Today_____
_____
_____

Today's NSP (What I want to improve) _____
_____

Today's Mind Program Affirmation _____
_____

What I didn't do today that I should have done
_____
_____
_____
_____

What I will Do This Week
_____
_____
_____
_____

What am I? _____
_____
_____
_____

Date:_____   Millionaire Daily Planner

My Long Term Goals

_____
_____
_____

Weekly & Monthly Goals_____
_____
_____
_____

What I Will Start or Do Today

_____
_____
_____
_____
_____
_____
_____
_____
_____
_____
_____
_____
_____
_____
_____

What I Will Stop Today_____
_____
_____

Today's NSP (What I want to improve) _____
_____

Today's Mind Program Affirmation _____
_____
_____

What I didn't do today that I should have done

_____
_____
_____
_____

What I will Do This Week

_____
_____
_____
_____

What am I? _____
_____
_____
_____

Date:_____   Millionaire Daily Planner

My Long Term Goals

_____
_____
_____

Weekly & Monthly Goals_____
_____
_____
_____

What I Will Start or Do Today

_____
_____
_____
_____
_____
_____
_____
_____
_____
_____
_____
_____
_____
_____

What I Will Stop Today_____
_____
_____

Today's NSP (What I want to improve) _____
_____

Today's Mind Program Affirmation _____
_____

What I didn't do today that I should have done

_____
_____
_____
_____

What I will Do This Week

_____
_____
_____
_____

What am I? _____
_____
_____
_____

Date:_____   Millionaire Daily Planner

My Long Term Goals

_____
_____
_____

Weekly & Monthly Goals_____
_____
_____
_____

What I Will Start or Do Today

_____
_____
_____
_____
_____
_____
_____
_____
_____
_____
_____
_____
_____

What I Will Stop Today_____
_____
_____

Today's NSP (What I want to improve) _____
_____

Today's Mind Program Affirmation _____
_____

What I didn't do today that I should have done

_____
_____
_____
_____

What I will Do This Week

_____
_____
_____
_____

What am I? _____
_____
_____
_____

Date:_____   Millionaire Daily Planner

My Long Term Goals

_____
_____
_____

Weekly & Monthly Goals_____
_____
_____
_____

What I Will Start or Do Today

_____
_____
_____
_____
_____
_____
_____
_____
_____
_____
_____
_____
_____
_____

What I Will Stop Today_____
_____
_____

Today's NSP (What I want to improve) _____
_____

Today's Mind Program Affirmation _____
_____

What I didn't do today that I should have done

_____
_____
_____
_____

What I will Do This Week

_____
_____
_____
_____

What am I? _____
_____
_____
_____

Date:_____   Millionaire Daily Planner

My Long Term Goals
_____
_____
_____

Weekly & Monthly Goals_____
_____
_____
_____

What I Will Start or Do Today
_____
_____
_____
_____
_____
_____
_____
_____
_____
_____
_____
_____
_____
_____

What I Will Stop Today_____
_____
_____

Today's NSP (What I want to improve) _____

Today's Mind Program Affirmation _____
_____

What I didn't do today that I should have done
_____
_____
_____

What I will Do This Week
_____
_____
_____

What am I? _____
_____
_____
_____

Date:_____   Millionaire Daily Planner

My Long Term Goals

_____
_____
_____

Weekly & Monthly Goals_____
_____
_____
_____

What I Will Start or Do Today

_____
_____
_____
_____
_____
_____
_____
_____
_____
_____
_____
_____
_____
_____

What I Will Stop Today_____
_____
_____

Today's NSP (What I want to improve) _____
_____

Today's Mind Program Affirmation _____
_____

What I didn't do today that I should have done

_____
_____
_____
_____

What I will Do This Week

_____
_____
_____
_____

What am I? _____
_____
_____
_____

Date:_____   Millionaire Daily Planner

My Long Term Goals
_____
_____
_____

Weekly & Monthly Goals_____
_____
_____
_____

What I Will Start or Do Today
_____
_____
_____
_____
_____
_____
_____
_____
_____
_____
_____
_____
_____

What I Will Stop Today_____
_____
_____

Today's NSP (What I want to improve) _____
_____

Today's Mind Program Affirmation _____
_____

What I didn't do today that I should have done
_____
_____
_____
_____

What I will Do This Week
_____
_____
_____
_____

What am I? _____
_____
_____
_____

Date:_____   Millionaire Daily Planner

My Long Term Goals

_____
_____
_____

Weekly & Monthly Goals_____
_____
_____
_____

What I Will Start or Do Today

_____
_____
_____
_____
_____
_____
_____
_____
_____
_____
_____
_____
_____
_____

What I Will Stop Today_____
_____
_____

Today's NSP (What I want to improve) _____
_____

Today's Mind Program Affirmation _____
_____

What I didn't do today that I should have done

_____
_____
_____

What I will Do This Week

_____
_____
_____

What am I? _____
_____
_____
_____

Date:_____   Millionaire Daily Planner

My Long Term Goals

_____
_____
_____

Weekly & Monthly Goals_____
_____
_____
_____

What I Will Start or Do Today

_____
_____
_____
_____
_____
_____
_____
_____
_____
_____
_____
_____
_____
_____
_____

What I Will Stop Today_____
_____
_____

Today's NSP (What I want to improve) _____

Today's Mind Program Affirmation _____
_____

What I didn't do today that I should have done

_____
_____
_____

What I will Do This Week

_____
_____
_____
_____

What am I? _____
_____
_____
_____

Date:_____   Millionaire Daily Planner
My Long Term Goals
_____
_____
_____

Weekly & Monthly Goals_____
_____
_____
_____

What I Will Start or Do Today
_____
_____
_____
_____
_____
_____
_____
_____
_____
_____
_____
_____
_____
_____

What I Will Stop Today_____
_____
_____

Today's NSP (What I want to improve) _____
_____

Today's Mind Program Affirmation _____
_____

What I didn't do today that I should have done
_____
_____
_____
_____

What I will Do This Week
_____
_____
_____
_____

What am I? _____
_____
_____
_____

Date:_____   Millionaire Daily Planner

My Long Term Goals

_____
_____
_____

Weekly & Monthly Goals_____
_____
_____
_____

What I Will Start or Do Today

_____
_____
_____
_____
_____
_____
_____
_____
_____
_____
_____
_____
_____

What I Will Stop Today_____
_____
_____

Today's NSP (What I want to improve) _____
_____
Today's Mind Program Affirmation _____
_____

What I didn't do today that I should have done

_____
_____
_____
_____

What I will Do This Week

_____
_____
_____
_____

What am I? _____
_____
_____
_____

Date:_____   Millionaire Daily Planner

My Long Term Goals

_____
_____
_____

Weekly & Monthly Goals_____
_____
_____
_____

What I Will Start or Do Today

_____
_____
_____
_____
_____
_____
_____
_____
_____
_____
_____
_____
_____
_____
_____

What I Will Stop Today_____
_____
_____

Today's NSP (What I want to improve) _____
_____

Today's Mind Program Affirmation _____
_____

What I didn't do today that I should have done

_____
_____
_____
_____

What I will Do This Week

_____
_____
_____
_____

What am I? _____
_____
_____
_____

Date:_____   Millionaire Daily Planner

My Long Term Goals

_____
_____
_____

Weekly & Monthly Goals_____
_____
_____
_____
_____

What I Will Start or Do Today

_____
_____
_____
_____
_____
_____
_____
_____
_____
_____
_____
_____
_____
_____
_____

What I Will Stop Today_____
_____
_____

Today's NSP (What I want to improve) _____
_____

Today's Mind Program Affirmation _____
_____
_____

What I didn't do today that I should have done

_____
_____
_____
_____

What I will Do This Week

_____
_____
_____
_____

What am I? _____
_____
_____
_____

Date:_____   Millionaire Daily Planner

My Long Term Goals

_____
_____
_____

Weekly & Monthly Goals_____

_____
_____
_____

What I Will Start or Do Today

_____
_____
_____
_____
_____
_____
_____
_____
_____
_____
_____
_____
_____
_____

What I Will Stop Today_____

_____
_____

Today's NSP (What I want to improve) _____
_____
Today's Mind Program Affirmation _____
_____

What I didn't do today that I should have done

_____
_____
_____

What I will Do This Week

_____
_____
_____
_____

What am I? _____
_____
_____
_____

Date:_____   Millionaire Daily Planner

My Long Term Goals

_____
_____
_____

Weekly & Monthly Goals_____
_____
_____
_____

What I Will Start or Do Today

_____
_____
_____
_____
_____
_____
_____
_____
_____
_____
_____
_____

What I Will Stop Today_____
_____
_____

Today's NSP (What I want to improve) _____
_____

Today's Mind Program Affirmation _____
_____

What I didn't do today that I should have done

_____
_____
_____
_____

What I will Do This Week

_____
_____
_____
_____

What am I? _____
_____
_____
_____

Date:_____   Millionaire Daily Planner

My Long Term Goals

_____
_____
_____

Weekly & Monthly Goals_____
_____
_____
_____

What I Will Start or Do Today

_____
_____
_____
_____
_____
_____
_____
_____
_____
_____
_____
_____
_____
_____

What I Will Stop Today_____
_____
_____

Today's NSP (What I want to improve) _____
_____

Today's Mind Program Affirmation _____
_____

What I didn't do today that I should have done

_____
_____
_____
_____

What I will Do This Week

_____
_____
_____
_____

What am I? _____
_____
_____
_____

Date:_____   Millionaire Daily Planner

My Long Term Goals
_____
_____
_____

Weekly & Monthly Goals_____
_____
_____
_____

What I Will Start or Do Today
_____
_____
_____
_____
_____
_____
_____
_____
_____
_____
_____
_____
_____
_____

What I Will Stop Today_____
_____
_____

Today's NSP (What I want to improve) _____
_____

Today's Mind Program Affirmation _____
_____

What I didn't do today that I should have done
_____
_____
_____
_____

What I will Do This Week
_____
_____
_____
_____

What am I? _____
_____
_____
_____

Date:_____   Millionaire Daily Planner

My Long Term Goals

_____
_____
_____

Weekly & Monthly Goals_____
_____
_____
_____

What I Will Start or Do Today

_____
_____
_____
_____
_____
_____
_____
_____
_____
_____
_____
_____
_____

What I Will Stop Today_____
_____
_____

Today's NSP (What I want to improve) _____

Today's Mind Program Affirmation _____
_____

What I didn't do today that I should have done

_____
_____
_____

What I will Do This Week

_____
_____
_____
_____

What am I? _____
_____
_____
_____

Congratulations, it has been 60 days and you will have seen amazing progress and many achievements in these past weeks. It is now time to up your game, get another planner at Amazon.com and keep driving your mind to bring you your every desire.

Please share this method with the people in your life you care about, they deserve their dreams too.   Remember to keep these planners, they are almost like a diary of sorts that you can look back on and trace your path from zero to hero. See how your real desires actually took better shape and allowed you to become more able to hit your goals and well on your way to complete success.

We would love to hear your feedback on twitter, tweet me at @sellerfinancing.

John Alexander

See my other books at
johnalexander.com/books

Made in the USA
Las Vegas, NV
14 February 2025

18021349R00037